GOD AND ELEPHANTS

Worship is a way of life for the believer; it is at the core of all we do as followers of the One so worthy of our devotion. **God and Elephants** *brings support development back to its core as a joyful act of worship. Looking back on our years as missionaries, praise wells up in my heart as I think of all the ways God has abundantly supplied our needs. This book will properly prepare your heart for the worship-walk to come.*

– Jeff Townsend (Staff Resource Specialist, ENTRUST)

There have been times when I have felt support raising was a necessary evil for anybody hoping to be a missionary—an obstacle that must be overcome in order to serve. **God and Elephants** *introduces a very different perspective, helping the reader realize that support raising is actually an opportunity for both individual and corporate worship. The focus and process explained in these pages can bring joy and life to a part of ministry that can be dull and difficult for many. This is a must-read for anybody whose ministry involves raising support, whether they are just starting or have been doing it for years.*

– Luke Wessler (Sports Friends Zambia)

God and Elephants is a refreshing perspective on the challenges of ministry fundraising. With humor, creativity, and practicality, Heather's Christocentric approach puts the emphasis where it needs to be but rarely is: learning how to effectively communicate personal stories of God's redemptive work as well as the inescapable call to abiding trust in His sovereign provision. This ought to be required reading for all support-based ministry agencies.

– Raul Cruz (Director of Spiritual Development, Saint Patrick Presbyterian Church)

Finally! A fresh book on prayer team building and support raising that gives several practical steps in a concise, easy-to-read format. The personal accounts told in God and Elephants will make you laugh, challenge your thinking, and point you to Christ as you seek His face to raise up a group of people who are committed to the Gospel going out. I personally have used several of the methods used in this book and have found it all extremely challenging, effective, and Jesus-honoring. Pick it up, read it and be blessed.

– Luke Voight (Sports Friends Malawi)

GOD AND ELEPHANTS

A WORSHIPPER'S GUIDE TO RAISING SUPPORT

HEATHER RICKS

ISBN-13: 978-0692272824

ISBN-10: 0692272828

To my amazing sons, Jeremy and Jonathan Ricks, I pray that you see God's hand on your lives and worship Him.

TABLE OF CONTENTS

ACKNOWLEDGEMENTS

AARON AND KELLY Bucy, you were willing to read my material when it felt more like a mess of ideas on paper. Thank you for your thoughts and insights that helped shape the end result.

Ruby Mikulencak, your contribution helped to impact the flow of the book in a big way. Thank you for your sincerity and your praise.

Raul Cruz, your words provided me with a greater vision and renewed excitement. Thank you for the gift of your knowledge and conversation.

Patricia Link, thank you for taking the time to read my first draft. Your loving marks of correction helped me to define a clearer direction.

Meg Ackley, thank you for your sweet support. You were the breath of encouragement I needed to keep going.

Carol Kejr, you're such a godly woman. Thank you for how you have continually come alongside me during my journey.

Dale Newby, thank you for your finishing touches. Everyone needs a bit of polish before being able to shine.

Erynn Newman, from A Little Red Ink, you made me laugh,

even when I saw all the red marks on the page. Thank you for using your gift for God's glory.

And I certainly can't thank my husband, Jason Ricks, enough. You were the one who wiped my tears when the going got tough, loved me through my doubt, and helped me to persevere. Thank you, Sweetheart, for always believing I can do anything.

FOREWORD

RAISING MINISTRY SUPPORT is a terrifying and daunting task for many, and can be one of the greatest barriers for some who have sensed God's call to missions. *God and Elephants: A Worshipper's Guide to Raising Support* is an excellent tool that equips those on this God-sized journey to tell their stories, resulting in an act of worship.

Different cultures around the world use stories, and who doesn't enjoy a good story? As someone who grew up in Nigeria and whose moral education centered on stories, allegories, proverbs, and parables, it's not often I find people who are adept at telling stories with impact. Heather is one of the few I've come across in my ministry journey. She's a master storyteller who, through this book, has graciously chosen to serve and equip others with her storytelling skills and her heart of worship, helping us see the support-raising journey in a whole new light. As she aptly puts it, "The support-raising journey is a unique opportunity for God to take center stage as you connect people with His work right here at home and around the world."

Throughout my ministry, I have written and read many prayer letters. Heather reminds us that we are not the center of these stories but are part of God's stories and the ultimate goal is worship.

As Joanna (my wife) and I commenced our journey of building relationships and raising resources for our ministry, I had no equipping, training, or instruction. We were stepping out on a new adventure of what was called foreign missions. Even more daunting was the fact that we were doing this in a context where raising missionary support was unknown. Since no one within our denomination knew anything about raising support, we were more or less a trial-and-error case. Complicating this was my own discomfort. By all standards, I was better paid as a doctor than most of the people I was asking to support me, and no one could understand why my wife and I, both doctors, would give up lucrative jobs and ask for donations.

I didn't understand my story as God's story, and I didn't understand support raising as an invitation to worship. In fact, worship was the last idea I would have considered in this process.

One day, I spoke in a local church about our ministry—where we were going and why we were going to a predominantly Muslim people group to use our God-given medical skills to share about Christ and His love for the lost. As I was leaving, a young man followed me outside. He was an engineer and what he heard had challenged him to reevaluate his own life and values. He concluded that he would like to use his engineering skills to serve God in world missions.

I was totally astounded. This young man didn't hear a request for money or a missionary asking people to get behind his ministry. He heard an invitation to recognize Christ's Lordship over his life and to surrender and worship Him. Here I was thinking that I was in church to raise support. I had no idea that sharing our story was, in fact, inviting others into an experience of worship and surrender.

Needless to say that young man changed my perspective. He brought me face-to-face with what Heather has carefully laid out in this book—God centered stories are an invitation to worship. I wish I had a book like this to equip and guide me as I set out on this journey.

Heather skillfully articulates what it is we are truly doing when we develop relationships and raise resources for ministry, helping us understand that both frontline ministries, praying and giving to support ministries, are acts of worship. Through a woven tapestry of God stories, she lays out amazing ways in which to recognize God at work and invite others to worship with us. She invites us on a journey of discovery of which the end result is a God-centered story, life, and ministry.

I highly recommend this book to all who have been called to labor in the harvest and all those who have been called to partner and journey with them. Together we join in the great worship and in the words of the psalmist: "Let the peoples praise You, O God; Let all the peoples praise You." (Psalm 67:3 NASB).

—Joshua Bogunjoko, Director of SIM International

I.

GOD AND ELEPHANTS

So whether you eat or drink or whatever you do, do it all for
the glory of God. *(1 Cor. 10:31)*

GOD GAVE ME an elephant moment. Red dust was
glued to my face with humidity as our family climbed
a ridge in the African savannah. With the chatter of
monkeys rising from the trees, I stayed close to our guide who had
a tranquilizer gun the size of Texas slung over his shoulder. We had
to hurry. We were on a mission—the elephants had been spotted.

As I stepped into the clearing, not even sure if the rest of my
family was behind me, our guide smiled and pointed excitedly to
his right. I had wanted and I had prayed to see an elephant in the
wild, but in those feeble pleas, nothing had prepared me for the
sight. When I turned my head, God flaunted the mightiness of
His creation on the stage of the Ghanaian landscape—just for me.
With breathtakingly graceful strides, three elephants walked past
and stopped right in front of us to graze on the trees.

Amidst their trumpeting calls, a splintering crack shook the calm as an elephant knocked over a tree with its head. This was real. A wonder I had only experienced through nature magazines and educational TV was happening before my eyes. I didn't want to breathe, afraid this moment would pass too quickly. The quivering strains of awe erupted into worship as I encountered God through the majesty of His creation.

In a smaller package, yet no less majestic, the glory of God came to life through the laughter of African children. Little faces with shy curiosity crammed beside me as each child fought to see their image on my video camera. Moments before, they had waved and giggled while I filmed them. Now they watched as they saw themselves perform on the tiny screen. Their eyes grew wide with excitement, and their reserve soon gave way to silliness. In a chorus of delight, they sang and danced in front of me, then ran back to watch themselves. They tugged my shirt to indicate they wanted more, and another round of laughter began. Many decided to participate, while others gathered to watch and cheer us on.

Though our languages were different, we communicated through smiles and clumsy hand motions. Cultural barriers diminished in the little village of Tumu, hundreds of miles from the city of Accra, Ghana where my family lived. In the giddiness of children, in their trusting hugs around my waist, I encountered God through the handcrafted beauty of His creation.

These pictures of Africa, along with countless more, cause me to desire, weep, hope, and laugh. These memories have one thing in common—they draw me into the presence of God. His artistry drips through tears, sings through roaring waterfalls and pounding waves, and radiates through handshakes, conversations, and smiles. All creation boasts of its Maker, acting as a pedestal for His glory.

Beneath the undercurrent of what the world screams, when everything else is whittled away, we were created to worship. That's it. Life happens at a rapid pace and threatens to suck us into its fury. When it's daunting, overwhelming, and suffocating, God makes Himself known through moments where He speaks in the nothingness of whispers or shouts in the winds of a hurricane. In that calmness, in that storm, nothing should distract us from our purpose of glorifying Him.

This understanding is the foundation for your support-raising journey. This voyage that lasts through the life of your ministry is not merely a task to perform as a means to get to the field and to get into ministry, nor can the focus be about money or building teams. Although these things are necessary and something to work toward, they are secondary objectives to a greater goal.

God is our provider. Rest in that fact. As we remain faithful to the task at hand by keeping our eyes fixed on the Creator, God's intent is to refine us so that we may be used for His glory. Along the way, we are simply called to worship.

As your journey progresses, it's strengthened by an ensemble of worship as others come alongside you to join in the work God is doing in and through you. What an exciting, yet daunting thought! You are accountable to those whom God has entrusted to you as partners and have been given the responsibility to continually connect them with God's work. You are called to be a worship leader—one voice— creating a chorus of praise to the Master.

You are the eyes to the mighty elephants and the ears to the laughter of children. Those undiscovered gems of God's creation and those moments that God is using to transform your soul are crying out to be discovered and experienced by those who may never set foot among the people you serve. Capture the delight, the storms, the majesty, the silence. God is in those moments.

Stories play a key role in helping people connect with God. They draw pictures, provide the voices to another world, and create experiences through which others can be involved. People want to participate by being given the opportunity to worship as God shows off through His creation and displays His work in miraculous and ordinary ways.

The purpose of this book is not to present another method for how and why to ask people for money. It's simply a tool to aid in developing and sharing your God-moments during your support-raising journey to ultimately draw others into the presence of God. When God is experienced and given His rightful place, worship happens. That's what your journey is all about. The rest is up to Him.

PREPARING FOR THE JOURNEY:

1. Spend a determined period of time (week, month, etc.), praying for your support-raising journey, asking God to prepare your heart and mind for the task He has given you.
2. Recruit a team of prayer warriors to pray specifically for you and your support-raising efforts.

Dear God,

I praise You for this journey of faith you've mapped out before me. I rest in the assurance that in Your perfect timing, You'll provide all I need and will nurture my relationships as I faithfully follow You. As I lay aside all other distractions, may all I do glorify You.

Amen.

II.

SURRENDER

But whatever were gains to me I now consider loss for the sake of Christ. What is more, I consider everything a loss because of the surpassing worth of knowing Christ Jesus my Lord, for whose sake I have lost all things. I consider them garbage, that I may gain Christ. (Philippians 3:7-8)

IT WAS SHRIVELED up, dead, and racing our car on thrusts of wind. As the tumbleweed trailed out of sight, I wished I could vanish as well. Wyoming was the closest thing to a frozen tundra I had ever seen, and my husband, Jason, and I had barely stepped foot into the state. We were traveling down I-80 to check out Laramie, the location of a possible church plant, when we passed a sign that read, "City of Buford, Population 2." Now, I'm an introvert, but that's a little sparse even for me.

Things didn't get any better. We crept along in the snow, following the faint tire marks of those who had previously traveled before us to the place where we were to meet our ministry team. When we arrived and opened our car doors to face this new place that vied to be our home, there was nothing around. I will define nothing—more tumbleweeds, a few scattered antelopes, snow, wind, and one building. I already had my answer as to whether or not we were going to move there. Umm, no.

Later, after we had arrived back in Cheyenne, Jason asked, "So, what did you think, Sweetheart?"

My reaction of crying was far kinder than my thoughts of punching him. I felt sad, lonely, and empty. Surely God wasn't moving us from the vast oasis of Portland, Oregon, where He had led us to plant an urban church, to a place where the bushes died and rolled around between the antelope. Not to mention we would have to live off support once again. I feared the only reports to our ministry partners would be, "We had nine prairie dogs, six antelope, and five people in church attendance today."

It wasn't until I submitted to the fact that God knew the desires of my own heart far better than I knew my own self, that I looked at the possibility of Laramie being the life-giving place it turned out to be. God simply called us to go. His still small voice took root in my heart until it changed my attitude from uncertainty to excitement for the people and ruggedness of the Wild, Wild West.

When our family pulled into Laramie, Wyoming on Halloween day, it was nine degrees below zero and dumping snow. I knew I was in for an adjustment—I think anything below sixty is freezing. If it hadn't been so cold outside, I'm sure the neighbors would've sat in their lawn chairs, sipped soda, and eaten popcorn while watching this little southern girl learn how to drive in the snow. I was proud it only took me two attempts to slide park into my driveway. Despite the things that could've quickly soured my opinion, God opened my eyes to His beauty in Laramie.

From day one, the community rallied around us and became our spiritual family. Side-by-side, we served unwed mothers, the homeless, and hungry college students. We sang in celebration as people came to know the Lord. My own personal tears of joy were shed as I watched my oldest son, Jeremy, be baptized in the local indoor pool—and, yes, snow was falling outside ... again.

God even brought us through the glorious sadness of seeing people leave as they followed after God to places beyond Wyoming. From the day God birthed that desire to move to Laramie until the day He moved us on to another ministry assignment, God displayed His faithfulness, showed how He provides, and demonstrated the fact that He holds the whole world in His hands.

If I had stayed in Wyoming for the rest of my days, I would've been satisfied. However, God continued to work in Jason and my life and challenged us with another step of faith. Our friends from Portland were moving to Tanzania and came to visit us before they left. As we reconnected and heard stories of how God was moving in Africa, I wasn't expecting to feel that ever-so-slight tug at my heart to move to Africa. But I felt it, and I wanted to scream, "No, no, no, Lord!" but agreed, instead, to take a trip to experience Africa firsthand.

Jason and I were continually warned not to be out in the streets of Kitale, Kenya past dark, but on one leisurely afternoon, the students invited us on a stroll to visit the market. As it turned out, I had a different timeframe in mind than what they had intended. With dusk quickly approaching, our Kenyan students were in no hurry to get back to school. They meandered through the market, stopping at every booth and perusing every trinket. They were comfortable. I was not and tried to keep the long walk back to school out of my mind.

Street children tugged my arm. A man grabbed me and tried to pull me into an overcrowded van headed to who knows where, and I had just been a stone's throw away from a shooting where I witnessed a man die. I was in culture shock overload. I said a quick prayer, telling God that if I ever made it back to school safely, I would never set foot in Africa again.

God has a way of stealing past my stubborn convictions.

It was the testimony of an African man that brought me to my knees before God in a willingness to follow Him, even to a place that scared me, in total abandonment. This man had just earned a degree at a biblical seminary in Kenya that caters to busy pastors, and he could not contain his excitement at the gift of knowledge he received. After coming to faith in Christ, he had immediately begun to share his faith, which eventually led him to pastor several churches. Lacking much understanding of the Bible, he preached the same simple message week after week, month after month. While many people came to a saving knowledge of Jesus Christ, this pastor wanted to disciple the people entrusted to him.

He learned about this school's program that would help him earn his degree while still being able to pastor his churches. He literally took what he learned at school each week and preached it from the pulpit on Sunday. Not only was he being transformed by his knowledge of God's Word, but his congregations were as well.

The need for discipleship is great in Africa. The eagerness to learn far exceeds any I have witnessed at home. It's a ravenous longing that brings the students early to class and keeps them up late to learn by candlelight. The seminary lacked teachers, and my husband had the gifting to teach them. Why not go?

As Jason and I, once again, surrendered our will to God's

and said our goodbyes to our friends in Laramie, God took our hands and led us directly into a storm. After God brought in most of our support and we were ready to move long-term to Dar es Salaam, Tanzania, nothing else went according to our plans. The team overseas fell apart, and as everyone returned home, we were unable to go. Stranded in Georgia with family, we had no income, no jobs, and a house we had already sold in Wyoming. The situation felt out of control, but God proved it was never out of His care. We watched in awe as He provided in ways I would've never thought possible. Many nights I wrestled with God, and tears soaked my pillow as I begged Him to make our journey easier.

He didn't. Making our journey easier wasn't part of His plan. Making me to be more like Jesus was always His intention. During this time, He gave me vivid applications of how to trust Him, and I can look back now and remember His goodness.

Four years after God first called us to Africa, we finally arrived in Accra, Ghana with a different agency. It wasn't the place we had expected to move, but it was the place God had intended for us all along. While in Ghana, we were able to experience God through Ghanaian students at Maranatha University College, conversations in the market, and even as our family walked through the treetops of a rainforest. None of these experiences would have been possible without our struggles. God used the weight of the journey to produce the jewels used to shine for His glory.

My story is different from yours. God has created you with your own desires, dreams, and gifts, and has tailored your experiences to shape you for His glory. If you're reading this book with the idea to give up a steady income and to live by faith, then I'll assume at some point in your life a longing to be used by God tugged you into your first steps toward obedience. You discarded security for a trust in a big God. You surrendered your dreams with a focus on eternity. In the culmination of those events, there's a story with people, places, ideas, longings, and needs that explains your passion to do the ministry God has called you to. It's waiting to be put into words and experienced by others so they, too, can hear what God has done and worship Him.

In a world that honors financial independence and boasts of tangible achievements and material possessions, a lot of people, including Christians, have a hard time grasping why anyone would choose to live in sole dependence on God for daily financial provision. When you're sitting in front of potential supporters, many will cock their head, pause as if searching for polite words, then manage only to say, "Now, tell me again, what this money is being used for."

The support-raising journey is a unique opportunity for God to take center stage as you connect people with His work right here at home and around the world. Therefore, the personal stories God has given to you should be the focus. Putting these God-moments into words helps potential partners understand your passion and the importance of joining God in His work. He stirred your own heart to pursue something greater. When you invite others into your moment of worship, there are opportunities for Him to stir their hearts as well.

The rest of this book will lead you through the steps of preparing and strengthening your stories in ways that help draw an audience's attention to God. As worship happens, the Holy Spirit will use these God-encounters to transform lives and build your teams.

PREPARING FOR THE JOURNEY:

1. Prayerfully reflect on your own personal story, journaling your thoughts and feelings when you have seen God at work.
2. Make a list of all the things—people, events, gifts, needs, etc.—God used to bring you to complete surrender to His call.
3. Praise God for how he has uniquely made you for the specific ministry He has called you to do.

Dear God,

I praise You because I am fearfully and wonderfully made (Psalm 139:14). From the beginning, You have crafted me with gifts and desires specifically tailored for all the things You have called me to do. Help me not to hold tightly to my own will, but may I surrender my all at Your feet, knowing I will gain so much more.

Amen.

III.
DOWNWARD, INWARD, OUTWARD

I WENT THROUGH A cross-stitching phase when I was younger. Embarrassingly enough, I didn't know one could be so inept at weaving a needle in-and-out of mapped out holes. My thread would often get knotted in massive clumps to the point where I couldn't even pull the loose end through. Scissors became my best friend. Many projects remained unfinished.

I'm not sure what made me think that cross-stitching a cute little bear for my mother-in-law for Christmas one year was a good idea, but I went through with the ordeal anyway. Somehow, by God's grace, I managed to complete it. Most people can proudly flip over their cross-stitch, and it's the same picture on both sides. I bought a picture frame so no one could see the mess on the back. The only hint of anything wrong from the front was a few stretched out holes and some bulges. Perfect. The next year I bought my mother-in-law a shirt.

Knowing the importance of worship is key to storytelling. It's a continual act that should be woven throughout the process, allowing the Artist to create a flawless picture for others to see and praise His name. No matter how the picture is flipped, it reflects the same inward and outward beauty.

Before you begin to meet with people, write your prayer letters and blogs, or speak in front of audiences, here are some helpful ways to prepare your stories with a heart of worship:

A. Live in awareness of God's presence.

The heavens declare the glory of God; the skies proclaim the work of his hands. Day after day they pour forth speech; night after night they reveal knowledge.

(Psalm 19:1-2)

The only usable toilet at the campground had to be bucket flushed, and there was a shortage of water. That alone, even without the swarming bugs with huge appetites, could have sabotaged my attitude enough for me to miss something glorious. As other distractions fueled my irritation, the church was gathering for worship in a pavilion located on a pristine beach on the Tanzanian shoreline. However, I didn't think much of the splendor. I thought of only the heat as I dragged myself across the blazing sand to join the others.

A slight breeze wafted through the rafters as I entered. Children raced through the chairs and played their games, and adults wandered in from their activities to find their places. Though the scene was chaotic, the noise was soon replaced with praise as the worship leader began to lead us *a cappella* in "God is So Good." We sang the chorus in four languages—Swahili, Afrikaans, French, and English—and an amazing feat happened.

In the moment where our voices rose above the swell of the waves, God transformed my heart with His magnificence.

I stood among other believers from different nations, worshipping the same God in four-part harmony. In that moment, I encountered God. I stumbled over the foreign words and probably mispronounced half of them, but God was glorified. Despite the sweat and slime, God freed me, and everyone else, from my grumpiness. God is so good!

God is everywhere and constantly at work. Things may not go according to our plans, but He holds us close and works in ways we may never expect. Live with your eyes wide open, astutely aware of God's presence. This alertness to Him is the threading of the needle and the downward stroke that begins the pictures that God is creating for others to see.

God is present in ordinary moments such as shopping in the market or driving the car. He may surprise you with a miraculous gift or speak through the wisdom of a friend. God-moments don't have to be blatant. As you recognize Him at work, capture these moments through stories so they can be used during the support-raising journey.

B. Be still before God.

He says, "Be still, and know that I am God; I will be exalted among the nations, I will be exalted in the earth."
(Psalm 46:10)

Ministry is a battle, and though invisible, tremors of the war are felt through busyness, idleness, apathy, pride, lust, disagreements, etc. All these sins fight to distort those beautiful pictures God wants to display through us. During the battle, God gives us one command. When the army attacks, while the arrows fly, we are to be still and know that He is God.

You must prepare your heart. Renew yourself daily through His word and continually equip yourself against Satan's sharpened sword. Being spiritually healthy is the inward work that aligns the needle in order to create the perfect picture. Nobody may ever see what's on the inside, but it's reflected in the outward image.

Before preparing the stories God has given to you, be in a posture of worship. It's only at this point of stillness and being in tune to Him that the Holy Spirit can speak through you to display those God-moments.

C. Lead others in worship.

Declare his glory among the nations, his marvelous deeds among all peoples. (*1 Chronicles 16:24*)

People are hungry to connect with God. This is when building teams and working toward deadlines have a greater purpose than the "How much can I put you down for?" mentality. You are building relationships with people who need to experience God in ministries beyond their scope, and God has placed you where you are for that purpose. Don't take this responsibility lightly.

God's wondrous deeds need to be declared among the people. As you live with awareness of God and prepare your own heart for the journey, pull the needle outward and let others see the beautiful picture God has created. In the support-raising journey, you'll constantly have opportunities to share God-stories through prayer letters, presentations, and blogs.

Whenever a story is presented to an audience, there is always some type of a response. Use these times to point people to God.

Preparing for the Journey:

1. Write down at least two ways you have seen God at work in the last month.
2. Come before the Lord, asking Him to prepare you for the journey that lies ahead.
3. Ask God to prepare the hearts of those who will soon hear your God-stories.

Dear God,

I praise You for all the beauty that surrounds me. No matter the circumstance, help me to keep my eyes trained on you in constant awareness of Your presence and how You are at work. I desire for my life and my words to honor You and to display to others those beautiful pictures of Your goodness You have so faithfully given to me.

Amen.

IV.
STORY TIME

Greater love has no one than this: to lay down one's life for one's friends. *(John 15:13)*

EVERY STORY OF the Bible unites to be one—the story of Jesus. Our Heavenly Father wrote the script of His relentless love that pursued a rebellious mankind in order to restore a perfect relationship. Mankind fell, a nation was born, and the Israelites wandered. Yet before the foundation of the world was spoken into being, God's plan was already set into motion. The prophets declared the coming Savior, and a baby's cry broke the silence.

Not once did God's love waver for us. The chant of God's chosen people, blind to their own faults, condemned Jesus to die for our sins. Nothing stood in the way of the Creator, who used the scars of His own Son to heal the wounds of His shattered creation. Through Jesus' death and resurrection, He conquered the grave so we could stand in perfect harmony with God once again.

It is finished. Our redemption is made complete, but the story continues.

Until the day that Christ returns, you're a part of the redemption story. The Church has been sent to the ends of the earth to declare the Gospel, and each one of your stories, no matter how great or small, fit into this bigger picture. When God is encountered, it's a moment to be shared with others so they, too, can experience a glimpse of the greater Story.

With this in mind, there is no wrong story if it points to God. He will use your words to move people regardless of whether you're an introvert with a fear of public speaking or if you lack creativity. However, there are some basic guidelines that can strengthen your stories and build confidence as you prepare to share these stories with audiences.

The ultimate purpose on the support-raising journey is to connect people with God. In order to fully engage your audience in worship, there are three main categories to consider when preparing your stories: what is effective storytelling, what is a God-story, and how do you create a God-centered story. It's important to understand the answer to each one.

A. What is effective storytelling?

Effective storytelling is the presentation of a well-prepared, God-centric story that conveys your passion and results in a response of worship.

To better understand this definition, it can be broken down into these four parts:

1. Effective storytelling is well-presented and well-prepared.

Prepare ahead of time. There is a difference between spending the necessary time in order to make your presentation powerful and throwing together something that's merely presentable. People in ministry have many demands on their time. As such, prayer letters, church presentations, support-raising opportunities, etc. are often viewed as a cumbersome duty in an already overfilled schedule. These things may come at inopportune times, but the fact remains that it takes time and effort to develop a story and present it well.

2. Effective storytelling is God-centric.

The "me" syndrome is a troubling epidemic that can creep into presentations without the presenter being fully aware of it. This most often happens when not enough time is taken beforehand to carefully craft a story in which God is the main character. Practicing your story ahead of time decreases the likelihood of rabbit-trails where you become the star of your own story.

Also, be careful not to abuse the "me" syndrome in prayer letters. The point of a prayer letter should be to connect people with God's work. The basic rule to remember is to keep God in the foreground, and let everything else point to Him. God is using you to do great things for Him. Lead others into worship out of that awesome thought.

3. Effective storytelling conveys your passion.

God did not walk you blindly down the path of raising support without creating you for your specific role. Out of His craftsmanship, He gave you desires and longings to be used for His glory. Understand your passion to do the ministry God has called you to do and allow the audience to experience it. With one taste of your excitement, desire can grow in others to be a part of what God is doing.

4. Effective storytelling results in a response of worship.

This may be the last part of the definition, but it's the most important aspect of effective storytelling. Leading others into worship is the climax that occurs when all the other three parts are combined. Effective stories allow the Spirit the freedom to do His part. Your job is to keep your focus on the right goal. Everything else will fall into place.

Use these four points of effective storytelling as a guide to create your God-stories. Throughout your support-raising journey, God has given you an unbelievable avenue to display the beauty of His work to others. Recognize that your God-stories are powerful, and make the most of them.

B. What is a God-Story?

Although people would know a story if they see or hear one, when many write or speak, anything but a story comes out. A list of facts or a sequence of events is often used in place of a

God-story. Both facts and sequences of events are necessary to establish a story, but they should never replace one. Simply put, God-stories happen when you dig below the surface to get to the heart of what God is doing.

Here are two examples to demonstrate the difference:

Example 1a – A list of facts and sequence of events: church presentation

> My name is Brian, and I spent the last two years in Ouagadougou, Burkina Faso, where my main role was a counselor at a boys' after school program. The program started out having just ten boys, but by the time I left, it had grown to about 45 kids. We met weekly for Bible study and to play games like ping-pong and football (soccer), and because of our relationships, many started coming to church ...

The above example may be true, but what happens when you use a story to paint a picture of what God is doing through Brian's ministry?

Example 1b – A story: church presentation

> My name is Brian, and I saw God move in mighty ways during my first two years in Ouagadougou, Burkina Faso. I'm a planner, so I thought I knew what to expect when I came into my role as a counselor in a boys after school program. Little did I know how

much God was going to use the unexpected to grow me and to build a stronger ministry.

Isaiah was one of ten boys who came when the program first started. Though he was drawn into the program by the ping-pong and the football (soccer) tournaments we played, he was reluctant to attend our weekly Bible study. This went on for several months, until one day, he heard me practicing French. No matter how hard I worked at it, my pronunciations were pretty bad. Thankfully, though it may have been out of pity, Isaiah offered to help. This was a gift from God.

This sixteen-year-old boy became my French tutor, and our relationship began to grow. While he taught me how to conjugate sentences, parse verbs, and pronounce words correctly, I began to share my own story with him about growing up without a mom. Isaiah's mom had died when he was only two. Through this connection, I was able to share with him about how Christ came into my life and filled that void.

Not too long after he began to teach me French, Isaiah started attending our weekly Bible studies and became a Christian. I've never seen anyone with such a hunger for the Word of God. Two years later, he is now one of our leaders and has helped us to grow our program from 10 boys to 45 boys who meet with us on a regular basis. He even makes sure that each boy has a way to attend a local church ...

The use of this personal story allows the audience to have a greater understanding of how God used the lives of two boys as instruments to spread the Gospel.

Example 2a – A list of facts and sequence of events: first prayer letter

> We are now missionaries! It has been three years in the making, but we finally did it. The mission agency, ABC, has accepted us after taking many tests—one of them a psychological test, thank goodness we're not loony!—and our plans are to head to Zambia by the end of July. John will be teaching math at an international school, and I'll be a physical therapist at a local clinic. In order to make all this happen, we need your support …

This doesn't explain their passion or how either of them came to the decision to move to Zambia. Take a look at the story that impacted their decision.

Example 2b – Story: first prayer letter

> John and I have always shared a similar passion— to abandon ourselves to the work of God no matter where it may take us. Since I have pretty much stayed in the same town I grew up in, God never challenged my sincerity until I encountered a little girl named Afia.

With disfigured limbs, Afia was a four-year-old little girl from Ghana who could barely walk or hold anything in her hands. Her adoptive dad carried her into my office and set her on the table. She had suffered a stroke when she was a baby, and her birth parents hadn't wanted her. Before her adoption, she had been living in an orphanage.

In just a few short sessions, I got Afia to sit up, take several steps, and hold a stuffed bear in her arms. She couldn't stop smiling at her accomplishment, and I haven't stopped smiling since. She changed my entire perspective on life. I knew God had something bigger planned for me—a plan for me to use my gifts on the mission field to show the love of Christ to children just like Afia.

John was on board with the idea to move overseas from the very beginning. God is now taking us to Zambia where John will use his gifts as a math teacher at an international school in Lusaka. Our target date to move is the end of July. You, too, can be a part of our journey. We need people who are willing to give financially on a monthly basis and to pray for us. Your support will help more little children like Afia to not only be given a chance to walk, but to encounter the love of God through the ministry God has called us to do …

This story helps potential partners to not only see their

heart, but also to see how their partnership could help spread the Gospel as this couple is used to show the love of Christ.

Through these examples, a story introduces the audience to another world and puts a face to the God-moments. The facts aren't missing; they are interspersed throughout the story. Use these examples to help you put words to the God-stories behind the facts and sequences of your own journey. They're there, and the audience needs to experience them.

C. How do you create a God-centered story?

An effective story has three essential characteristics—a central theme, a hook to get the listener interested, and a strong finish. Each part is examined with the purpose of making God the center of your stories.

1. Stories need one central theme.

What would happen if you tuned into a cooking show, and when the chef was explaining how to make chocolate chip cookies, she began to talk about the ingredients for sesame chicken? Then, as she was sifting flour into the cookie dough bowl, she explained how to make homemade noodles the right consistency? Not only would that be frustrating, but you may also end up with chocolate chip cookies with a hint of soy sauce. My husband will tell you I don't need any more distractions in the kitchen when I'm trying to cook.

Having a central theme means the story must carry one main idea throughout. The chef may have lots of knowledge about cooking other foods, but a half hour show is not the time to brag about everything she knows. She must start with the concept of how to make cookies and keep that same focus until the they come out of the oven. That's how her audience will know how to make the perfect cookie.

This idea is not new; however, it's a concept that's often abused. When given a set timeframe, many people attempt to cram their entire life history into their presentation. When presenting in this way, a five-minute presentation can sound like this:

> I grew up in a Christian home, and at age 5, I became a Christian. I learned a lot of Bible stories and loved going to church. However, while I was in high school, I started hanging out with the wrong crowd, and this caused me to walk away from my faith. I got into things that I wasn't supposed to, like drugs and alcohol, and found my self-worth through my boyfriends. My dad died when I was sixteen, and that sent me into a deep depression, because of which I needed lots of counseling. It wasn't until college that a friend of mine led me back to Christ, and I was excited about God once again. At age 30, I had the opportunity to go on a mission's trip to Haiti with my church, and this is where I felt God calling me into missions …

What is the central theme of the above paragraph? When she became a Christian, walking away from her faith, drugs and alcohol problems, self-esteem issues, her dad dying, depression, or a mission's trip to Haiti? As you may have realized, there isn't one central theme. This is just a list of events that have happened in this girl's life. All this information makes it hard for the audience to understand the actual purpose of her presentation. Any of these themes can be turned into a great testimony with stories, but you must choose a singular theme, make it the focus, and expound on it.

Since you're raising support and learning about how to connect people with God's work, ministry should be the primary theme of your stories on this particular journey. If other past experiences can be used to strengthen the ministry focus, then use them as support. Look at the same girl's testimony when ministry is used as the central theme to explain why she's pursuing missions:

> The brokenness of Haiti was far deeper than the outward destruction caused by the earthquake. I went this past summer with my church for the rebuilding efforts and came back with a greater understanding of how God could use my own experiences to reach through the buried hurt and introduce people to my loving Savior.
>
> The first Saturday I was there, God connected me with a fourteen-year-old girl. Though she considered herself lucky because both her parents and two sisters survived the earthquake, she didn't know how to cope with the loss that surrounded her. She had been introduced to drugs and alcohol before the earthquake. Now she depended on them in order to cope.

Though worlds apart, my story was similar to hers. I, too, used drugs and alcohol as a teenager. For me, it was to numb the pain of low self-esteem. My devastation didn't come through an earthquake, but it blindsided me in the form of a car accident that killed my dad. No amount of counseling seemed to bring me from the depths of depression. Only when I was reintroduced to my loving Savior when I was in college did I break free from the bondage that had enslaved me for so many years.

My wounds are now healed, and God used my testimony to speak into this girl's life. She prayed for Jesus to be her Savior and for Him to take control of her grief. A local lady named Ritha has taken this girl into her care and continues to pour the love of Christ into her.

I once thought I was a failure, but God picked me up out of the ashes. He used my past brokenness and pain as a bridge to reach this girl, and I knew I wanted to continue to do the same for others. I am now pursuing a counseling degree with the hopes of using it for advancing God's Kingdom in Slovakia with ABC agency ...

With the second example, please notice that the story was not centered on her alcohol abuse or her dad dying. These events in her life shaped why she is going into ministry; therefore she used them simply to show her passion for ministry.

When giving a support-raising presentation, not all of the events in your life need to be included. If a particular life experience doesn't fit, then shed the unnecessary content and use only those that helped shape your decision to follow God's call.

Below is an example of a man named Greg who is going to Ethiopia to disciple Christians. When he was younger, he experienced the death of his best friend and overcame bacterial meningitis as a child. Both are powerful stories; however, when he prepared a presentation for a local church, they were not needed. He had many other stories that better described his passion for his particular ministry. Here is an excerpt of his presentation, keeping ministry as the focus:

> I wasn't expecting to be a missionary. In fact, ever since I was young, I had my whole life planned out. I was going to go to college, get a seminary degree, marry a beautiful woman, buy a house, and have 2.5 kids. However, my life was interrupted, gently but earth-shatteringly, by the still small voice of God whispering to my heart through a five-year-old girl from Ethiopia. She's my adopted sister, Abby, who came into my life when I was 17.
>
> I didn't know anything about the world beyond America, or Tennessee for that matter, and was in for an abrupt education on life. Abby didn't know one word of English when we brought her into our home. She spoke only Oromo, the language of her Ethiopian village. In order to relate to her, I began to study about Ethiopia and to learn her language. The whole family got involved, and soon, I found myself falling

in love with a country I had previously only known to exist on a map.

My perspective of the world changed. As Abby began to sing songs and ask questions about Jesus, I couldn't help but think of all those from her, mainly Muslim, village who needed to hear the Gospel. I wanted to help, but I just didn't know how ... yet.

I continued with my plan for my life, until years later, after I had graduated seminary, the opportunity arose to go on a mission trip to Ethiopia. God was asking me to lay aside everything and make myself available to be used by Him. While I was working with pastors in the capital city of Addis Ababa, God made my purpose for being in Ethiopia clear.

I met a pastor named Dawit who was from Abby's same village. This was no coincidence. Dawit had only been a Christian for three years. He was attending the pastor's conference to gain more training and tools to reach his village.

All I could do was smile at how God works. Years earlier, He had kindled my desire to reach others in Ethiopia through my sister Abby. Now God was revealing the bigger picture. I had the tools and education that were needed to help pastors like Dawit reach their villages. All along God had been equipping me and guiding my steps for His plans ...

This story is centered on God directing Greg's steps toward Ethiopia. The only time he may choose to use his other past experiences is if his audience needs to hear them. For example, if he is speaking to a group of people who have overcome adversity, he might begin his presentation by saying, "When I was younger, I survived bacterial meningitis and the death of my best friend. Because of these events, I mapped out my life and worked toward goals with fervor …"

When preparing your presentations, remember to include only stories that will show your audience how God used these events to lead you to your ministry.

2. Stories need a 'hook.'

Hooks are interesting words or phrases used at the beginning of stories that immediately draw your audience into the story. In the specific environment of your support-raising journey, hooks are the catalysts for your God-moments and should, first and foremost, begin at the point of the story that draws your audience's attention to God. To begin the process of writing a hook, there are two things to think about: your story and your setting.

a. Think story.

Too many times people get up front, make an introduction, and start giving a business report, or they begin a prayer letter with a step-by-step account of the past few months. Although God can use this, it isn't fully utilizing the tools He has given in order for His greatness to be displayed. To resolve this dilemma, first think of a story that could be used to help the audience understand how God is moving.

Here are some questions to help you think of the right story:
- For your initial support-raising efforts:
  * How did God stir your heart for this particular ministry/country?
  * What excites you the most about this ministry?
  * What experiences in your life directed you to your present opportunity?
  * How can you show a glimpse of God at work in this ministry/country?
  * What specific needs are you fulfilling?
  * What did your point of surrender look like?

- For your regular prayer letters:
  * How are you seeing God move in your ministry, through people, and in His creation?

- For your meetings with supporters when you're back from your ministry:
  * How did you see God move?
  * What will the future look like for your ministry?

There are stories behind each of these questions. Think of the moment when God entered your story, and begin your hook from that moment.

The following are two examples to demonstrate the difference between using a hook as opposed to not using a hook:

1a. Non-hook:

My wife, Jane, and I are moving to New York City in a couple of months to work at an inner-city church called Hosanna Bible Church. I'll be the youth pastor and will help a little with their music ...

1b. Hook: Think Story – What circumstance led them to pursue ministry in New York?

My wallet was stolen ten years ago when I was on a trip to New York City. After all this time, I didn't expect to get it back. However, God surprised me by using this event to open the door for me to work as a youth pastor at Hosanna Bible Church in New York City ...

2a. Non-hook:

I love my job as a Kindergarten teacher at Hope Academy in Niger. I have 11 students in my class from 6 different countries. My favorite thing to do with the kids is teaching them Bible stories ...

2b. Hook: Think Story – How did she see God at work?

A little girl dumped a half bottle of glue in her hair, a little boy ate a box of crayons, and the class turtle escaped because he was left out of his cage. This all happened in just the first week of me teaching at Hope Academy in Niger. When things seemed to be at their worst, I learned how God can use the mouths of babes to speak mightily to adults ...

Each of these hooks gives a glimpse of how God is moving by drawing the audience into the story.

b. Think setting.

In what setting will you be sharing your story? Hooks may look different while meeting with someone one-on-one or while in a smaller group setting, but they're still needed. For a casual setting, practice the hooks to your God-stories so they segue your conversation seamlessly into your presentation. Otherwise, you could end up talking life for two hours, leaving only five minutes to say you're going into ministry and you need partners to join with you on this journey. You never want to hurry a presentation. It's best to talk life afterward.

Here is an example of how to use a hook in a coffee-shop setting:

1a. Non-Hook:

Hey, man, it's great to see you again. Thanks for coming to hear about my new ministry opportunity in Ecuador. I want to show you some pictures of our recent trip. Here's Sally standing in front of the new church we helped build. They were meeting under a tree for a while before that. Here's me with some of the guys from the church. This one is the pastor. He has a real heart for the community ...

1b. Hook: Think story – How did God work to bring this family to Ecuador?

> Hey, man, it's great to see you again. I appreciate you taking the time to meet with me and to learn more about my new ministry opportunity in Ecuador. I want to share how, just a little over five months ago, God gave Sally and me the opportunity to visit, and we came back with our lives changed.

> While I was in Ecuador, God spoke to me during my quiet time and gave me a desire to serve among the Ecuadorians. I had never thought about leaving my ministry position in Virginia, so I told God I was willing to serve if He opened the door. Before Sally and I left, Rev. Hernandez pulled me aside. He told me he had been praying for a new worship leader, and after working alongside me, he thought God was leading him to ask me. Isn't God amazing that He answered my prayer that quickly …

The above example demonstrates how a hook can lead into the story, even in a one-on-one setting.

In writing, hooks can look different. Here is an example of how to use a hook for a prayer letter:

2a. Non-Hook:

> In November, missionaries from all over Peru traveled to Lima for our yearly renewal conference. This is a

time where we rest from the busyness of life, recast our vision, and bond with our fellow co-workers in Christ …

2b. Hook: Think story – What experience at the conference impacted her the most?

"One God. One family. One purpose." God used these words, written in bold letters across the classroom board, to not only set the tone for our yearly renewal conference held in Lima but to also change my attitude …

With this one phrase, a picture begins to develop as to how God worked in this woman's life at the conference.

The purpose of a hook is to create interest for the story. Therefore, hooks must relate to the story. A joke is not considered a hook because it doesn't draw an audience's attention directly to the story. A story should display your personality and can be humorous; however, make sure the focus of your presentation is how God is moving and not keeping the audience in stitches.

Once you have taken time to think of a particular story and to construct your hook, you must finish your story.

3. Stories need a strong finish.

In a support-raising presentation, you shouldn't tease people with a hook, and then wait to tell them how the story ends. When the mood for worship has been set, don't interrupt it.

To finish a story, answer whatever question you raised in the hook.

Hook 1 question: How did God use a stolen wallet to lead him into ministry?

Hook:

> My wallet was stolen ten years ago when I was on a trip to New York City. After all this time, I didn't expect to get it back. However, God surprised me by using this event to open the door for me to work as a youth pastor at Hosanna Bible Church in New York City …

Answer:

> Julio Acosta was the man who robbed me all those years ago, though I didn't know his name at the time. The police caught him for a different crime, and he went to prison for eight years. By God's grace, he experienced the transforming love of God through a prison ministry. When he got out of prison, he planted a church in the same community he grew up in so he could share Christ with young people.

One day, while his mother was going through his stuff, she came across my wallet that still had my ID in it. She gave it to Julio, and Julio wanted to do the right thing by giving it back to me. Little did he know that when he called, I was seeking God's direction as to what steps I would take next in life. Julio told me his testimony, and we instantly connected. He had an opening in his church for a youth pastor, and I knew God was prompting me to fill the need ...

Hook 2 question: How can God use the mouths of babes to speak mightily to adults?

Hook:

A little girl dumped a half bottle of glue in her hair, a little boy ate a box of crayons, and the class turtle escaped because he was left out of his cage. This all happened in just the first week of me teaching at Hope Academy in Niger. When things seemed to be at their worst, I learned how God can use the mouths of babes to speak mightily to adults ...

Answer:

By Friday morning of the following week, I was exhausted and began to doubt my ability to teach a class of eleven kindergarteners from six different countries, all of whom have a lot of energy. In fact, I began my quiet time that morning by asking God,

"Why in the world do you have me here?" Well, He answered.

That day, six-year-old Makayla, a child of a missionary family from Australia, gave me a handmade book she had written as a gift. Inside, she had drawn an image of her holding my hand and another of us at the foot of the cross. Her story read, "God gave me you. I learn about Jesus." That was all it said, but God used those words and pictures to refocus my attention on the reason I had wanted to come to Niger in the first place. I wanted to love on these children and teach them about Jesus ...

These two examples display how God is working through their lives and ministries. Each of these stories uses details that create feelings, describe the setting, tell what happened through actions, and continually point to God. Make your own stories come to life through details. The rest of the presentation will flow out of this.

Stories engage people at a heart level. Set aside the money, the deadlines, and, for many, the awkwardness. Focus on the bigger picture. Worship the God who guided your every step. Asking people to join your teams will flow naturally out of this worship. As you begin to think through the God-moments in your life, God will open the doors to the audiences with whom you'll share your stories.

Preparing for the journey:

1. Think of a specific story of God's work in your life and ministry.
2. Write a hook for your story.
3. Use details and facts to finish your story.

Dear God,

I praise You for sending Your only Son to die as a penalty for my sins and to restore perfect fellowship with You. Thank You for giving me my own stories that are a part of this bigger Story. In the busyness of work and ministry, help me to understand the importance of using the unique avenue of the support-raising journey to share Your mighty works so others can be drawn to You.

Amen.

V.

AUDIENCE

All the nations you have made will come and worship before you, Lord; they will bring glory to your name. For you are great and do marvelous deeds; you alone are God.

(Psalm 86:9-10)

A. Have the right focus.

Your audiences will be at all different stages of life and spiritual maturity. Only God knows each individual's heart. Your role is simply to set the stage for the Spirit to work by keeping all eyes fixed on the true Provider. If you keep your mind and attitude focused on money and how much people should give, then you are trying to take control. Relax. It's the Holy Spirit's job to prompt them to give.

Don't be discouraged if you don't see immediate results or if the initial momentum has stalled. You never know the true impact of the words God has given to you. If worship happened, then

God was glorified. Keep working hard, and He will take care of you.

B. Prepare for each audience.

Too often people treat their presentations with a "one-size-fits-all" attitude. They scribble it out and deliver a canned presentation for every audience. You might get away with this in many instances, but you likely will not connect with your audience on a heart level. Your purpose is to lead them into worship, not to rush to the next task. Before putting pen to paper, you should consider three things about your audience that will help you shape your presentation.

1. What will be the size of your audience?

The size of a group gives a different feel to your presentation. When speaking, will you be in front of:

a. A large group: Congregation, Conference
b. A medium group: home gathering, men/women's group, Sunday school class, Bible study group
c. One-on-one setting: Coffee shop, individual's home

The smaller the setting, the more intimate the presentation will be. You obviously will not bring your stories and read them word-for-word when having coffee or dinner with someone. Instead, in an intimate setting, casual conversation will be your guide. However, know your presentation and stories well enough that they flow out naturally. This puts you in the position to not only guide the conversation, but also to easily answer questions.

In a larger setting, where the audience may not know you, you'll have to do formal introductions and use stories that can relate to all different types of people. Adjust your presentations accordingly.

2. What will be the setting for your audience?

a.   Will your setting be formal or informal?
– Dress appropriately: You don't want to wear jeans and a polo shirt to a church where men dress in suits and ties and women wear only dresses. You may have to call ahead in order to find out the proper dress code. Neither men nor women should let their attire be a barrier to worship.

b.   Will your setting be inside or outside?
– Prepare mentally: Outside, there may be distractions like wind or a noisy playground you have to take into account. Satan will try to use anything to block worship. You will not be able to prepare for everything, but the more you learn about the location, the more comfortable you'll feel when giving your presentation.

c.   Will your setting provide all the needed equipment?
– Be prepared: Pack your own equipment, cables, batteries, etc. You don't want to be thinking about finding a cable five minutes before you're to speak.

3. What is the demographic of your group?

a.   Is your audience composed of believers, unbelievers, a mix?

– What happens if a group of neighbors throws you a going away party and asks you to share why you're moving? What a perfect opportunity to explain your passion and point them to Christ. Be wise in your choice of stories, and don't use Christian lingo they will not understand.

  b.   What is the age of your audience?
– The age of the audience makes a huge difference as to what stories and language you'll use. You want to be respectful of an older audience, and in turn, you don't want to speak over a younger audience's understanding.

  c.   What cultural background is your audience?
– When your audience consists of people from another country, you may not be able to create a complete picture in their minds by using American lingo. If they don't understand, they can't fully worship.

  d.   Are you presenting in front of people you know or don't know?
– This changes the feel of your presentation. If you are speaking in front of an audience who may not know you, remain sincere and open, yet speak more formally with less casual conversation.

Invest in your audience. God has placed them in front of you in order for His wonderful deeds to be declared. Understand their uniqueness and prepare accordingly.

PREPARING FOR THE JOURNEY:

1. Make a list of potential people with whom you would like to share about your ministry.
2. Pray through each individual name on that list, asking God to prepare their hearts.
3. Invest in the relationships with the people God has given to you.

Dear God,

I praise You for specifically choosing my audiences. Cultivate in them a heart that's eager to hear and willing to participate in all that You're doing. Ordain the time we have together in order for the stage to be set for the Holy Spirit to do His work. Above all else, I pray for the lives of many to be transformed as they hear of Your marvelous deeds.

Amen.

VI.
USING YOUR STORIES

IN THE FIVE-YEARS Jason and I served in Laramie, Wyoming, I experienced an abundance of God-moments. Sharing a meal with our spiritual community every week, sitting across from college students and hearing their stories, serving side-by-side with our church as we raked leaves and cooked for our neighbors, mountain biking at Tie-city with my family, and bouldering in Vedauwoo (Vee-dah-voo) state park with friends—these are just a few snapshots in which God was present and moving in my life. Each one has stories I can use to point an audience toward God.

As you have learned in the previous chapters, you are on your own personal journey in which God is working in ordinary and miraculous ways. These moments have helped shape the person you are today. Hopefully, you've been thinking through how you've seen God at work and the steps of telling your story. Now that you have these stories, how do you use them during the support-raising journey to build and maintain your support teams?

Here are some ways to incorporate your stories in every step of the support-raising journey.

A. Your Initial Support Presentations

There's a lot of footwork involved before you meet with people, but once you have your meetings set-up, the process of writing the presentation begins. Although each presentation will look different for each audience, presentations should have the same basic information. Below is a general format of a presentation in an outline form, and a short example of a presentation is provided at the end:

PRESENTATION OUTLINE:

Presentation Outline:
  I. Introduction
      A. Introduce yourself and family.
      B. Thank your audience for taking the time to hear about your ministry.
      C. Transition statement
          1. Tell where you're going.
          2. Use it to flow into story.
  II. Story
      A. Use a hook.
      B. Finish the story.
          1. Married couples should each share their own stories.
              a. This demonstrates that both spouses are passionate about the particular ministry opportunity.

        b. This allows the spouse to highlight his or her own ministry from a firsthand perspective.

   3. You can use multiple stories depending on the timeframe provided.

        a. If a married couple is given five to seven minutes to share, one short story each normally fits into that timeframe.

        b. Practice ahead of time so you're respectful of the time.

III. Body

  A. Include the needed facts

   1. Give the country or ministry area to which God is leading you.

   2. Describe your ministry position.

        a. What is the ministry opportunity God has called you to?

        b. Why are you needed?

  B. Tell about the organization/ministry through which you will be going.

   1. Who are you going with?

   2. Why did you choose to go with them?

  C. Answer all the questions your audience will want to know. Examples may include, but are not limited to:

   1. How long do you plan to live in _____?

   2. What language do they speak?

   3. What are you currently doing?

   4. What will your spouse be doing?

   5. What will the children do?

6. What is your favorite thing about the ministry/ country?

7. What will your housing situation be like?

8. What will the food be like?

9. Where will the children attend school?

IV. The Closing

A. Give the call to action.

1. Give your target date for leaving.

2. Ask the audience to join your prayer and financial support team.

a. They need to know how they can join God at work.

b. Be bold.

c. Tell them where you will be located after you finish talking, so they can connect with you.

B. Tie back in the opening story.

C. Summarize your thoughts.

Effective Presentation Example

For those of you who don't know me, my name is Dan, and it's great to be here today. I appreciate you taking the time to listen as I tell you about the ministry God has called me to do in Monrovia, Liberia and present the opportunity for you to be a part of it.

Intro

Transition Statments

The knowledge that God gave my mentor, Tate, became the difference between life and death.

Hook

Complications during a routine surgery had already pushed it an hour longer than anticipated, and Pan, a nineteen-year-old man, was losing more blood than the clinic had in supply. He was going to die, and as a last effort to save his life, the doctor had to get him quickly from the remote Asian village to the nearest hospital in the city, which was a two hour drive down winding mountain roads.

Tate was their lifeline. He lived in the city and had the connections and knoweldge needed to make the transition happen quickly and smoothly. Minutes mattered. Pan was slipping fast. Tate set up an emergency plane to carry the patient to the hospital, and within twenty minutes, Pan was being loaded aboard. Tate even called ahead to the hospital, so when Pan arrived, he was able to go immediately into surgery. Due to such wisdom and fast action, his life was saved. Pan was back home just three days after his ordeal.

This was just one of the stories Tate told me that God used to impact my own life. God had used Tate as a missionary in Asia for nearly twenty-seven years. He wasn't a doctor, pastor, or a teacher who I always believed were superheroes where, in

Finish the Story: What was Tate's Knowledge/Why did it matter?

one swift act of mercy, they could change a life forever. But Tate had an important gift like mine. He was an administrator who worked behind the scenes to ensure that everything ran smoothly.

STORY CONCLUSION

After hearing his stories, I knew Tate was a part of a team that worked together toward a bigger goal. I never felt I had the giftings that screamed missionary, but at that moment, God opened my eyes to how I could use my gifts on the mission field as well.

ABOUT AGENCY/WHY HE CHOSE THEM

As I began my quest to be a missionary, I felt comfortable with ABC agency the moment I walked in the door. They were like family to me, and their passion was to share the love of Christ with the nations. It's working. They're in 50 countries on four continents. Many of the groups they work with have never even heard the gospel. This excited me. I had a lot of countries I could choose from in which to use my gifts, but I first pursued a placement in Asia where Tate had lived. It's a place of mountains and skiing, something that, being from Montana, was important to me.

WHAT HE WILL DO

However, God had something else in mind. The team from Monrovia, Liberia heard I had applied, and after I was accepted, they asked if I would pray about moving there to be the hospital administrator. Not only would I be representing the hospital, but I would also be managing the personnel, finances, and facility. This would involve me keeping on top of all the governmental requirements—which can change from day-to-day in Africa. God created this job description perfectly for me.

There was just one thing standing in my way—I would have to get used to the idea of the hot climate in Liberia. Today, I checked the weather report for Bozeman, Montana. It was 17 degrees and snowing. I also checked the weather report for Monrovia, Liberia, and it was 92 degrees with a chance of rain.

Needless to say, God did an amazing feat in my life to move this snowbird who loves to ski to a place on the beach that has never seen snow. I researched Liberia, and the more I did, the more I fell in love with the country. They eat a lot of chicken and rice and spicy foods, and their national sport is football/soccer. I love chicken, and I love to play soccer. I could see myself starting to fit in. I have always wanted to be available to God and His leading, so I was willing to make sacrifices. Since the compound where I'll be living is on the beach, maybe I'll learn to surf.

My faith date to move to Monrovia is set for the end of July. That's only five months away. They have been without a hospital administrator for almost a year now. Although they have someone filling that position temporarily, that person is leaving in August, and I would like to have a month to train under them.

I'm very excited about the chance to serve God in Liberia and want to give you the opportunity to be a part of the ministry He has called me to. There are two ways for you to partner with me. First, I need a team of people who are willing to be my prayer support. I'll be sending out regular prayer letters and prayer updates. Please sign up in the back if you're willing to be on this team.

I also need a group of people who are willing to come alongside me financially. It's by faith that I'm stepping out to move to Africa, but I have financial needs that have to be provided before I can take those first steps. If you feel the Holy Spirit leading you to give to my ministry, either on a monthly basis or for my one-time start up costs, please complete the information cards, so I'm able to contact you personally. I also

ANSWERS THE QUESTIONS

TARGET DATE, NEED

CALL TO ACTION

have information about how to give online and a card with our specific cost estimates for you to prayerfully consider giving toward. I'll be standing in the back to answer any of your questions.

Just like Tate who worked behind the scenes to save Pan's life, I can't wait to be able to tell you the amazing stories of the things God is doing in Liberia. Thank you again for having me today.

This presentation includes all the elements needed for the audience to see how God worked in his life and to allow them to understand how they can participate in the work that God is doing.

B. Home Presentations/Missions Conferences

My brother got quite the surprise when he opened his gift from me on Christmas morning. I tensed with anticipation when he unwrapped it, because I knew he would love the present and would play with it all the time.

The wadded paper was cinched together with layers of scotch tape, which made the unwrapping tedious. I couldn't wait to see his reaction—he nearly gave up. To this day, I still don't know if his response was of disappointment or relief when he finally unraveled a tiny head and said, "Oh, there they are. I was wondering what happened to them."

Weeks before I had slipped into his room and snatched several action figures off his dresser. I was beside myself with joy for finding such a perfect gift. They were some of his favorites, so I knew he would love them. The gift was practical, economical, and fun. I couldn't go wrong. Even as a seven-year-old, I was already thinking with a missionary mindset.

Your stories are a gift. One of my favorite things about working in the home office of our mission agency was being able to hear the stories of the missionaries returning from the field. Hearing their updates reminded me of the importance of the job I was doing on the home front, and it renewed my passion for my position.

Your partners need that same gift. Don't shortchange them by grabbing something off the shelf and handing it to them in wadded paper with too much tape. You have the unique opportunity to shatter stereotypes and redraw a world that has been sketched by media and ignorance. God is at work. His deeds are mighty, and His creation is beautiful. When you come back home to speak, churches and ministry partners need their eyes focused on the God of the nations. Give them the stories that hold that knowledge.

EFFECTIVE PRESENTATION EXAMPLE

For those of you who don't know our family, my name is Martin, this is my wife, Gayle, and we have two children, Nick is nine and Wendy is seven. Thank you for inviting us to be here today and for allowing us to tell you about how God has been working in our family's life while we've been living in Nigeria for the past five years.

> **TRANSITION INTO MARTIN'S STORY**

INTRO

HOOK

As a doctor, I see both tragedy and success on a daily basis. Often, I may never know what happens to my patients once they leave my care, but this past November, God gave me a gift by allowing me to see the impact of my work through a man named John.

When John returned to the hospital to greet me, it had been over a year since I treated him, and I, honestly, didn't remember him at first. He had malaria, something I see on a regular basis, and he was strong and back on his feet sooner than most. I see hundreds of patients a month, so he was quickly forgotten as I moved ahead with each day's tasks. But I had impacted him. The one thing I always do before I treat a patient is pray with them and introduce them to Jesus, the only one who can truly heal them.

In my routine I had done the same thing with John, and he accepted Christ that day. What I didn't know was, after he left the hospital, he had gone back home with a deep desire to learn more about this Jesus he had encountered. He traveled to another village near his own where he knew a missionary lived and was discipled by him. As his knowledge of the Lord grew, he began to reach out to his friends. Today, there are ten believers in his predominantly Muslim village that John led to the Lord. They meet in his house every Sunday, and I recently had the opportunity to worship with them. I was moved by their deep love for God. They're seeing the hand of God move as He works mightily among them.

When I moved to Africa five years ago to work at ABC hospital, I committed my gifts to God as a means to share the gospel. Most of my days are a normal routine of patient rounds and paperwork, but I can never take for granted how God uses someone like me in the scale of His greater plans. The people are hungry for God and eager to hear about the One who loves them unconditionally. I praise Him for allowing me to play a small part in John's story and the lives of the others to whom I get to minister.

While John works at the hospital, I'm more than just a stay at home mom who home schools Nick and Wendy. I mend scraped knees, play host to the neighborhood kids, and lead a women's Bible study.

TRANSITION INTO GAYLE'S STORY

HOOK

In the midst of all these things, I have witnessed the same miracle happen three times in a row.

God has given me the amazing opportunity to minister to a group of women from the village every Tuesday night, and they have challenged my faith through the strength of their prayers. Four of the seven ladies have husbands who are farmers and who depend on God to bring both the rain and the sun. Our village has been in a severe drought for nearly three years, and each time the crops were planted, it was time to watch those women in action. They fasted and held all-night vigils to pray for rain to water the seeds.

Being an American who puts her security in a backup plan, I asked a lady named Jacoba what they would do if the rain didn't come.

She said matter-of-factly, "I don't worry about such things. God will provide."

And He did. The morning after each prayer vigil the storm clouds gathered across the horizon until rain broke loose to drench the thirsty land. Sometimes it would last a day or two; one time, the rains lasted an entire week. It never stopped until there was adequate rain for the seeds to take root. I witnessed this miracle happen three times, and these women never doubted.

We worship a God who hears each and every one of our prayers, and he cares enough to provide for the livelihood of African farmers. I have learned to pray both big and small prayers, but most of all to pray with faith that God is working and sovereign.

Over the last five years, we've watched our family grow in ways we weren't expecting. We've had two dogs, five chickens, and one goat named Thomas. On the human side of things, Nick and Wendy have made several close friends that we consider part of the family. The neighborhood kids gather at our house every day to play, and many have started calling us Mamma Gayle and Pop Martin. They know they'll always be loved and accepted at our house, and God is opening up so many doors to share Christ.

I went to Africa five years ago without a ministry title, but in the end, I have strengthened the relationships with my own children, become a mother to many more, and have found new sisters in Christ with whom I journey. That means more to me than any job in the world.

We have truly lived the truth that God is everywhere. I saw Him at work in John's life as he fell in love with Jesus and grew a community of believers that have become strong in their faith. Day to day, we see God at work in the lives of our children, and He even allows us to witness miracles. Thank you for being on this journey with us. We couldn't do it without you.

There really is no set way to give a presentation just as long as you have God in the forefront. Remember to use stories in order to help engage your audience, because when their attention is fixed on God, worship happens.

C. Initial Invitation Letter

If you desire to meet with people face-to-face or in small gatherings in homes, the best way to introduce your prospective partners to your new ministry opportunity is through invitations. Once you send the invitations, then you follow up with a phone call. This makes it easier, because if people receive invitations before you call them, then it's not a cold call. When people know the reason for your call ahead of time, the conversation will be more comfortable for both of you.

A sample invitation with a story may look like this:

Dear Chris and Emily,

I hope things are going well for the two of you. I want to share a ministry opportunity God has opened for me.

A year ago I sat at a table with a young teenage mom who had been abandoned by her family. She felt hopeless and had nowhere she could turn. Through a mentoring program I participated in last spring, God allowed me to be a part of her story as I shared with her about the hope I have in Christ. That day began my journey to help others like her. I'm now a part of XYZ ministries in Chicago, a nonprofit ministry that provides shelter, food, work skills training, and, most of all, the love of Christ to teenage moms.

I'm going to be in your area on __(dates)__ and would like to set up a time to talk more about this ministry and how you, too, can be involved with helping girls encounter the amazing love of God. I'll call you on __(date)__ to set up a specific time when we can meet together.

Please be in prayer for our time. I'm looking forward to seeing you again. Thank you.

Paige

A story in an invitation gives them a taste. When you sit down with them face-to-face, you can give the bigger picture.

D. Prayer letters

A couple came to our church one Sunday and talked about how they were going to Asia. Jason and I didn't know them, but their presentation stirred our hearts to give on a monthly basis. We signed up for their prayer letters and received the financial forms. We were ready to go! After two years, but rarely hearing anything about their ministry, we directed our support elsewhere. We wanted to be involved with what God was doing in Asia. That's why we started giving in the first place.

Do you see how vital a tool prayer letters are to your support-raising ministry? You can't neglect the teams who give financially and pray for you. That's why it's a team. Your relationships don't stop when you get on the plane. You need to continue to nurture them and connect them with God's work.

Journaling is an important step of the prayer letter process. When you encounter God moving in your ministry and life, write these times down. This habit is beneficial for several reasons. First and foremost, you'll always have a record of God's greatness, and as you look back, your journal becomes a book of worship. Also, when months go by between prayer letters, it can be difficult to recall particular stories. However, if you write them in a journal, the potential material to use for your prayer letters is already there for prayerful consideration.

When it comes time to write your prayer letters, please realize the difference between a news blurb and a God-story. The main purpose of your prayer letter is to connect people with God's work. If you just want to highlight the news that little Timmy took his first steps, then use social media and blogs. However, if you want to use little Timmy taking his first steps as a God-moment, then you might use it as a story like this in your prayer letter:

> Working with the Inuit people over the past five months has been an incredible blessing. It has stretched my understanding of who God is and how He works in other cultures. Just last week I watched my son, Timmy, take his first steps. He clung to the edge of the coffee table while taking a stiff-legged stance. With his eyes fixed on me, he freed his hands and took three wobbly steps in my direction. Though he fell soon afterward, his determination led him to keep trying until he could move freely around the house.
>
> My son gave me a great picture of how I, too, have learned to trust my Heavenly Father while I have lived hundreds of miles from my home in the Canadian Arctic. My first steps in this different country were wobbly—the first dog sled I made fell apart and left me stranded until my caring adoptive family came to my rescue. God has continually placed people in my life who have helped me learn to walk securely under

His guidance even when things were unfamiliar. I
have learned how to stomach eating walrus, been
shown the depth of community through communal
sharing, and grown in my knowledge of God through
silence in a way I never expected …

God is in the everyday moments. This person could've done
a whole story around the fact that his dog sled fell apart and
how he saw God in the people who rescued him, or he could've
told of his first time eating walrus with the new community
surrounding him. He chose, instead, to use his child's first
steps to give an example of his own Heavenly Father and son
relationship. There are no wrong stories just as long as God is
the focus and it speaks truth without embellishment.

E. Blogs

Blogs can be entertaining. They're a fun way to share everyday
glimpses of what life is like, and people enjoy reading about
those things. However, remember that you're representing God
and your agency/ministry/church. Be careful about what you
post. There's no need to vent or to say only grim things about
your host culture. Beauty is everywhere. It's always a good idea
to have an extra pair of eyes to read what you write to make sure
your writing won't be taken offensively. If you have any doubts,
it's best not to post it.

F. Social Media

Social media is a great way to give day-to-day updates, showing what God is doing through your ministry and directing people as to how they can participate. However, don't use these conveniences in place of your God-stories in your prayer letters or presentations. Not everyone sees these news blurbs, and many would rather connect with God through a more significant means.

All these examples are simply to be used as guidelines to help you understand how you can connect people with God through your own God-stories. The main point is to make God's work come alive so others can actively participate in His goodness, and all of these tools provide an opportunity to worship.

PREPARING FOR THE JOURNEY:

1. Set up your support-raising appointments.
2. Prepare a presentation for each specific audience.
3. Practice your presentation until you feel comfortable sharing it.
4. Pray for God to help build your teams.

Dear God,

I praise You for being able to give the gift of stories so others can experience You. I desire to share each of them with an attitude of praise and thanksgiving. Out of a heart of worship, please build my prayer and financial teams and strengthen my relationships. You alone are worthy to be praised.

Amen.

VII.

IN THE END

Therefore, since we are surrounded by such a great cloud of witnesses, let us throw off everything that hinders and the sin that so easily entangles. And let us run with perseverance the race marked out for us. (Hebrews 12:1)

NO PROMISE CAN be made during the support-raising journey that, by following certain steps, everyone will have all their money raised by a given deadline. Be diligent, take action, and work toward your goals. That's biblical. However, don't let cultural expectations redefine truth. Nowhere in the Bible does it say that God works according to our timetables or the goals set by man. God isn't worried that your prospective ministry will fall apart without your presence. Paul never made it to Spain, but that doesn't mean his mission was a failure. I'm absolutely certain God still shared His gospel in Spain.

God is doing a work in your life to prepare you for ministry. The support-raising journey is an act of faith that God uses to transform us into His likeness. That's the bigger picture. For many who are diligent, God will move swiftly and miraculously. For others who are diligent, He may choose a winding desert lane with little light. Neither way is wrong. God has a path designed specifically for you so you'll learn, first and foremost, how to cling to your Provider.

Jason and I have seen both high and low points on our support-raising journey. God has blessed us with an out-pouring of money. On our way to be full-time missionaries in Dar es Salaam, Tanzania, God led a stranger at a church we spoke in to give a check for ten thousand dollars toward our ministry. When God changed our course to work with a different agency in Accra, Ghana, we had lost our momentum, and raising support had become an uphill battle.

Even after the initial thrust to get into ministry, the support-raising journey still takes work. Our journey continues to have both plentiful and meager times. During a particularly difficult storm in our life with health issues and weighty medical bills, Jason and I lost, yes lost, a total of about eight hundred dollars in monthly support in one weekend and three consecutive phone calls. However, God, in His goodness, brought in what we needed to keep us sustained.

Everything is under God's control. God uses these difficult times to stretch our faith and to teach us to depend solely on Him. Due to the lessons we have learned through the hardships, I wouldn't have chosen any other path. Our greatest takeaway from both the good and hard times—as we continue to do our part and strive toward the goal, we always see God's provision.

In the end, no matter what happens on your own personal journey, the only thing that matters is if you glorify God. He will lead you to mountaintop experiences and carry you through difficulties. Along the path He is taking you on, you are simply called to worship. Continually recognize God at work around you, personally pursue Him, and sacrificially lead others into His presence. Regardless of the results, you'll be successful. With perseverance, work hard, and keep running the race marked out for you. He will guide your steps. Along the way, surrender your own plans to God and bow in worship to Him.

PREPARING FOR THE JOURNEY:

1. Praise God continually for providing, no matter how that may look.
2. As you are on this journey, recognize the ways God is refining you to be like Jesus.

Dear God,

I praise You for being my strength as I persevere on the race You have marked out before me. As I make plans and work toward goals, may I continually lay everything down as a praise offering to You. I acknowledge that You are my true Provider and take comfort in the truth that You are with me through all my circumstances. Refine me, O Lord, and use me for Your glory.

Amen.

VIII.

SUGGESTIONS FOR RAISING SUPPORT

THERE ARE A number of approaches to raising support. Here are some practical ideas to aid your journey:

Prayer

Prayer is the foundation upon which your support-raising journey should be built. Begin on your knees, and build prayer teams to be mighty warriors for your ministry. It might be helpful for you to think of your prayer team in three categories.

- General Prayer Team: These are all the people who have signed up for our prayer letters. In each letter you'll provide prayer requests and praises to keep them informed and to guide their prayers for your ministry.
- Weekly Prayer Team: Invite everyone on your General Prayer Team to partner with you by committing to pray

for you at least one particular day each week. Send out brief prayer and praise updates on a regular basis, keeping them informed as to how to pray for you and your ministry.

- Intimate Prayer Team: Personally ask a small group of trusted friends from your Weekly Prayer Team whom you can go to when facing difficult or sensitive issues to be a part of this team. As needs arise, ask this group to pray for specific seasons of life and ministry.

List-making

Write down everyone from your past and present who may be interested in hearing about the ministry opportunity God has given to you. Ask your parents and friends if you can contact anyone they know who might be interested in your ministry opportunity as well.

Set up all types of appointments:
- Face-to-face meetings – These casual meetings are great for nurturing relationships. Meeting one-on-one with people can reach them at a deeper heart level.
- Home gatherings – Ask friends and family if they would be willing to open their homes and invite people in order for you to present your ministry.
- Church groups/classes – In addition to your own contacts, ask friends and family if you can speak in front of their classes or Bible study groups.
- Larger group settings –These are general audiences such as congregations or conferences and are helpful in reaching a broader audience. It's best to follow-up

the contacts you make from these with face-to-face meetings.

Building your financial and prayer teams is primarily about investing in people. In our seventeen years of raising support, Jason and I have personally found that smaller, more intimate settings—like coffee shops, dinners, and small gatherings—provide the best opportunities to make significant connections with potential partners. Often, travel is required. This isn't necessarily convenient, but it's worth it. Carving out time to engage with people will bless both them and you.

Goal setting

Set personal goals to work toward, recognizing that God is the One who is ultimately in control. Setting goals helps you to keep focused on the task at hand. As you make goals by faith, make them attainable to succeed. Praise God when you watch Him move you toward success.

Accountability

Choose a trusted friend to hold you accountable for setting goals and following through with appointments. If the journey gets hard, use him or her to help you see the refining work of God in your life. God may be choosing to use your difficult circumstances to grow you. Allow him or her to speak truth into your life.

Expectations

Expect God to move. He is big and doesn't allow you to walk this journey alone. Wait in eager anticipation of seeing God's greatness even when times get tough.

Invitations

For face-to-face meetings, send out invitations a few weeks in advance of your arrival in a particular city, inviting people to meet one-on-one with you. The invitations should state the purpose through a story and list a date in which you will call them in order to set up a meeting. Be organized and call on the day you listed.

Church and Other General Audience Presentations

Don't discount the importance of speaking in churches, Sunday school classes, or any other kind of large group setting. People need to hear about the work God is doing. You may be pleasantly surprised by who will give when you let the Holy Spirit speak through you. Ask pastors if you can speak to their congregations. Also, ask friends and family if you can speak to their churches, Sunday school classes, and small groups.

Audience Specific Presentations

Prepare your presentations for each specific audience. Use this as an opportunity to worship.

Timeliness

Please be on time to your appointments. This sets the mood.

Preparation

Come to each appointment with the proper items—needed equipment, brochures, ministry information, sign-up sheets, financial information, updated prayer cards, pictures, etc.

Follow-up

For everyone who signs up to be a prayer or financial partner, make sure you follow up with them through phone calls, face-to-face meetings, and even notes. Send a personal thank-you note to every financial and prayer partner. Continue to send personal notes to those who are a part of your teams throughout your journey.

Diligence

God gives us the privilege of joining Him as He builds our support teams. Raising support may get you out of your comfort zone, but you have to trust God to lead the right people to be a part of your teams. Keep praying for God to give you opportunities to share and to help others worship Him. Don't shy away from letting others know what God is doing. Opportunities to share your stories can happen at any moment.

Perseverance

Sometimes it's hard not to feel discouraged when you're working hard, and your support reaches a peak and stops. Reflect back on the journey God has led you on and praise Him for being faithful. He's still at work. He may have different ways to grow you. Keep working toward your goals, and God will guide your steps.

AFTERWORD

Dear God,

I praise You for all the memories You brought to mind while I was writing this book. As I reminisced, I was continually brought to my knees in awe of Your faithfulness and provision. I praise You for that gift. My prayer for those who read this book is that this journey doesn't become just another task to perform. I understand how daunting the support-raising journey can feel and how it can easily become just another check mark on a to-do list.

Ease their fear and reluctance, and help them not be motivated by dollar figures or deadlines. Please show them that the greater purpose in all of this is simply to encounter You. May they be led into worship as they recall the memories You lay upon their hearts and, in turn, be excited about leading others into worship.

Thank You for uniquely crafting their journeys as You refine them to be like Your Son. I boldly ask that You bring the right people before them who will be thrilled to join You in the work You're doing. Build their teams through Your mighty strength. You don't promise the journey to be easy, but You do promise to be with us. In the end, may they have glorified You in everything they do.

Amen.

ABOUT THE AUTHOR

Jason and Heather Ricks were married in 1994, and they dedicated their lives to serving God, making themselves available to minister anywhere He led them. Though their prayer of dedication was sincere, Heather quickly realized that God's plans looked different from her own. They were continually called to abandon traditional paychecks and to trust God to provide support through others. At one point Heather prayed, "God, I know there are ministry positions that provide a salary. Just once, could you please lead us in that direction?"

However, throughout this journey, Heather's faith has been strengthened as she has seen God provide even during the bleakest times. Every trial has proven that God is trustworthy. This humbling revelation led her to worship her Heavenly Father in deeper ways.

After coming home from Accra, Ghana, Heather worked in the training department of their mission agency. This experience combined her passion for telling stories with her new zeal for training missionaries. Her desire to help others worship God throughout the support-raising journey grew out of this newfound love.

Contact information:
Web site: www.godandelephants.com
e-mail: heather@godandelephants.com